T H E P

S E R I E S

Series Titles

Bowed As If Laden With Snow
Megan Wildhood

Always a Body
Molly Fuller

Silent Letter
Gail Hanlon

New Wilderness
Jenifer DeBellis

Fulgurite
Catherine Kyle

The Body Is Burden and Delight
Sharon White

Bone Country
Linda Nemec Foster

Not Just the Fire
R.B. Simon

Monarch
Heather Bourbeau

The Walk to Cefalù
Lynne Viti

The Found Object Imagines a Life: New and Selected Poems
Mary Catherine Harper

Naming the Ghost
Emily Hockaday

Mourning
Dokubo Melford Goodhead

Messengers of the Gods: New and Selected Poems
Kathryn Gahl

After the 8-Ball
Colleen Alles

Careful Cartography
Devon Bohm

Broken On the Wheel
Barbara Costas-Biggs

Sparks and Disperses
Cathleen Cohen

Holding My Selves Together: New and Selected Poems
Margaret Rozga

Lost and Found Departments
Heather Dubrow

Marginal Notes
Alfonso Brezmes

The Almost-Children
Cassondra Windwalker

Meditations of a Beast
Kristine Ong Muslim

Praise for
Bowed As If Laden With Snow

"This is a collection of poems that places no illusory limitations upon apocalypse. From the private tragedies of a single human heart, to the burning finish of our planet, no wrenching change is beyond the piercing mission of these poems. With a poetic voice as incisive as it is devoted, Megan Wildhood gives unwavering honor to what falters and dies—and with this, she offers hope in radical accompaniment with whatever may befall us."

—Candace Tkachuck
reparational activist and writer

"For Megan Wildhood, life hasn't gone unnoticed. I like to read poets for their imagery and the places they take me. But Megan. She's different. Her writing grabs me by the arm, spins me around, and sets the big lumbering mass of my revolving world to rotating on a whole new axis. Her insights into life are personal and deep, consistently showing me hidden, perhaps forgotten, truths—many of them tricky, sticky truths that other writers might prefer to leave untouched. By her poems I'm not just moved, but transported, transformed."

—Don Haggerty
poet and painter

"Megan is the storyteller of poets. Her work draws you in, commands attention, and knits an enigmatic yet cohesive web of nature, grief, and the human condition. I've worked with many writers over the years and I've never come across a voice as unique. The echoes of truth and circumstance within these pages will move you as the tide . . . in, out, and to every edge—luring you ever deeper."

—Katherine DiZio
Creative Director and Designer

"Megan Wildhood's collection of poetry deftly explores the relationship of humanity with and within the environment of nature and our planet, Earth. Notes of smallness versus greatness, despair versus hope, and the nature of love and hate come together in a symphony of chords, both dissonant and harmonious. Upon each reading, something new is gleaned."

—Michele Cacano
Lead Facilitator of The Seattle Writers Meetup

BOWED
AS IF
LADEN
WITH
SNOW

poems

Megan Wildhood

Cornerstone Press
Stevens Point, Wisconsin

Cornerstone Press, Stevens Point, Wisconsin 54481
Copyright © 2023 Megan Wildhood
www.uwsp.edu/cornerstone

Printed in the United States of America by
Point Print and Design Studio, Stevens Point, Wisconsin

Library of Congress Control Number: 2022949264
ISBN: 979-8-9869663-7-3

Cornerstone Press titles are produced in courses and internships offered by the
Department of English at the University of Wisconsin–Stevens Point.

DIRECTOR & PUBLISHER   EXECUTIVE EDITOR
Dr. Ross K. Tangedal   Jeff Snowbarger

SENIOR EDITORS
Lexie Neeley, Monica Swinick, Kala Buttke

PRESS STAFF
Ellie Atkinson, Hannah Fenrick, Patrick Fogarty, Angela Green, Cal Henkens, Brett
Hill, Julia Kaufman, Amanda Leibham, Maria Scherer, Abbi Wasielewski

For my late grandparents, whose love for me shapes so many
of these poems,

and to the friends who have become, through time or trial,
chosen family

Poems

This Glass Ledger

progress of petal, blushed like a clapping hand,
plates a sun gleam.

how does a world hold you?

unrequited lash from calloused palm
closed around a belt.

stones puncturing stream,
catching footfalls, sure and not.

careening car spun out in a slosh,
shaky hands wring the scene.

ceaseless sun strike, fragile, frosts
the night tine between once-friends.

chesttights, dusk tips its hat to the pidgin
spoken between light and dark, full breaths.

Procession

If you follow a human through an ocean to the bottom
      of the ocean not the human
you will find things that have been there forever maybe
      calcium carbonate polyps and life that doesn't need light
      but can definitely die
and you will find things that will be there forever
      descendants of synthetic polymers made of
      phenol and formaldehyde
      so no wonder they don't die
and it will be sad but that's why you take a human
      though their kind did the sad thing
it will also be like you are a kid again
      they are smart enough to be in awe of everything
      over and over
and you won't notice the pressure
air is really heavy like sand or a soul
is maybe the air sad
and isn't it weird how creatures
      humans
so finite that were you to follow one to the end
      of herself
      you'd still have enough time to see the oceans
            what you can see of them
            them and not what our hurting systems put them up to
can make such permanent things
      the only way to remain is to never be alive
            and so never have to die?

Remainder

Heaven and earth will pass away...No one knows about that
day or hour, not even the angels in heaven, nor the Son, but
only the Father.
—Matthew 24:35-36

The Jewish uprising against the Romans
in 70 AD: the final end-time battle.
Coins were minted. The world remained.
A French bishop announced the end

of the world in 365. The world remained.
Three learned men said, no, the year 500
will be the last because of the dimensions of Noah's Ark.
Pope Innocent III: the world will end 666 years

after the rise of Islam. After their leader's 1260
prediction failed, the followers of Joachim of Fiore
rescheduled the end of the world to 1290
and then again to 1335. The world remained.

1346–1351: Black Plague: end of the world for many.
Some people who were alive around 1439 thought the world
would end. Hand-wringing: now that people no longer had
to remember anything, now that everything could be written

down, what will become of everything we love?
People feared books would destroy culture.
The world filled with tomes and remained.
Now imagine a democracy without a free press.

A Puritan minister declared the end three times,
starting in 1697. John Wesley said anytime between
1758 and 1836. Rural farmer and Baptist preacher
William Miller promised The End in 1844.

The world remained and everyone was disappointed.
The Catholic Apostolic Church, founded 1831,
couldn't give an exact date for Jesus's
return, just that it would be when the last

of its founding members died, which was 1901.
1939 turned out to be a good candidate for the end.
The world remained.

Jim Jones saw visions of a nuclear holocaust
occurring in 1967, which the current
administration says you can survive.

"You can live in remains," they mean.
A doctor of natural medicine and founder
of a Ba'hai sect: Halley's Comet will obliterate

Earth in April 1986. The world remained. His friend:
a series of disconfirmed prophecies that would lead,
step by step, to the apocalypse. Also: Middle

Eastern terrorists would attack New York
with nuclear bombs. The world remains.
A quatrain by Nostradamus, who survived

the Plague, says the "King of Terror" will
come from the sky "in 1999 and seven months."

Y2K. 2012. Some think 2016.
Some 2020. Some think the Internet

will yet destroy everything.
The world remains.

The world remained. The world remains.

Perhaps the world will start to end the moment people no longer d

Until the last hour, the world will remain.

Mystery Confirmed

By the end of the year my grandmother was born,
there were two theories about very small things
and both were right.
The previous year, there had been none.

The thought experiments turned into very small,
very precise machines. Think it, it becomes.

    the very act of observing something changes it

Some things are too long to see:
radio waves, the whole truth,
the end of the rainbow of history,
even if everything is consciousness.

If everything is consciousness, then who is thinking:
bombs bring peace? whiteness is better? trees are paper?

    observation is transformation

If seeing something changes it,
who should step in front of a mirror?
Who should watch a murder?
Who can be let into a peaceful meadow?

And who needs to turn their gaze away
lest we leave but a quiet spot

    before we see what's going on?

Cementation

A saturated sky fell apart over our pasture:
snow's big reach gathered us all like a mama hen
for those five eventides before the strong-armed storm
gentled back to our usual terse wind and endogenous wet

that bears us so much. We broke fruit for the first time
that year much later than usual, then continued to
note the peace or distress of each parcel
of land, placing bets, hopes, for next season.

Next season brought Caterpillars and men in yellow
with personal stop signs to burn
their two-lane ribbons through our uneven fields,
their machines stumbling as they blunted our harvests.

We swatted at black dust. We coughed into cupped hands
or paisley bandanas. We held vigil for the buried bugs and
blades of grass, kneeling with our mother beside the husks—
insect, crop, meadow, way of life.

Timber

The US is the fourth-largest exporter of forest
products in the world: $9.7b in 2015.
Ergo: money does grow on trees.
Indeed, it is made of their bodies.

Ergo when a tree falls in a forest,
the trees will hold a moment of silence
for one of their own whether any human
is around to hear it or not.

And there are not always humans around.
But we cannot then say ergo, we are alone.
Our belief that we are is our fallenness;
ergo, accepting embeddedness is us righted.

Honey Bees Dance Their Science

Ladies, get in formation, we're going to warm up together:

The world saving is up to us. Rise up with me, twirl all the way.
Follow me—let's shimmy out our tour of the facilities.

Shake those honey makers! But save the sexy, pointy bit
for the ultimate…you know. Waft those beautiful face arms
all over the threat, getting its dimensions and trimensions

and did I mention to wait? Wait, lovelies, until you are sure
it's coming for our home. Flowers? You'll instinctively feel
their defenses. Well, except those the squeaky giants
put up around them—you know I mean fences.

Those glorious bull's eyes covered in pearlshine?
The shinier, the sweeter. They're asking to be licked
up and down
and through by you and you and you, sisters.
In every color!
Don't be shy! I know it's rough out there,
having so many of us die,
but when those giant hands

start to swat, just bust a move and your sisters

will know
what to do. It's not worth giving up the last half

of your precious digestive tracts just to attack
any old puny giant.
Trust the guidance your face arms
If you think you smell
even a hint of something,
you're smelling something.

My babies, come home before dark but, if you can't,
look up and watch how
all that light goes crisscross
and remember all that your mamas

told your body hairs—
if the light goes right, it's all right.
Home is a glistening saunter past the brittle cornfield
where giants
spray their chemical versions of nature
but you all know, my ladies,
that not one thing can replace us.

Windier is better—
moving things are easier to count—
and clouds are no match
for that delicious UV light.
Don't bust a gut defending the home
unless your tongue
tells you you'll kill the trespasser, too.

We'll all rush to the scene because none of us should die alone.
But even I've been sucked into thinking I could save the sacrificed
one if I gave up my abdomen's end, too. My Lord, my sisters,
do we stick and sting and stay and sway together!

Share the flowers—
when you find the delectable ones,
give us an elancer or a loop-de-loop
so we can all take notes and pass on the knowledge.
Weeds, too.
They're tastiest but the giants have loaded
them with bee killer.
They don't know, yet, dearests, that, if we go, they go.

Ready? Identify your targets, take your bows, and let's hit it.

Sundays

Heaven lost its sheen in a room
that smelled like a dentist's office,
so sterile it stung your throat.

Termagants taught us with lumpy felt
cutouts the stories of bread loaves,
extra fish and enemies, the Velcro

sounding like kissing every time
they needed to relocate a sheep
or endangered infant king.

Miss Angela was the only teacher
whose hard eyes were gems rather than stones.
I let her stroke my hair during snack time,

where they introduce you to eating animals
by doling them to you—a small circus line up—
in Dixie cups. The boys bit all the heads off

and spread their little massacres across the table
to the girls' side, getting excused for playtime, stealing
kisses, without having to clean up the mess.

Clay

When we played all those blue games near the highway,
Mom didn't stop us at first, though cars
flowed like the creek behind our house.

When we knocked over her favorite pot
of daisies on our rush
after a runaway soccer ball, then Mom dashed,

overtook us. Cars stop, now,
and have to claw their way
through a snagging siren.

Maybe this moment
is the moment,
friends suggest years later,

that I got my guardian angel. Maybe.
The stream still
has to use its teeth to get by.

Green Room

I used to think a green room
was where jealous people went
for a timeout.
You could slay some dragons, travel
time, sleep with a prince, skydive, save the world,
whatever it took for you to learn to want the life you have.

There Are Limits

Aspen green.
All the trees are in the sky
reigning down in ash browning out the eye

like apples. Candy red.
Plastic blue.
Exhaust black.

Mountain purple.
Beheaded like popped
blackheads.

Whitehead. Fire yellow
line in the sand
of history. Caution yellow. Are we at the timberline of
history?

Timber lines. Headwaters green.
Tongue blue.
Whole fields of it; tiny tongues.

Earth color.
Multi-potentialed.
Greed black.

Greed blue.
Greed green.
Greed orange—sand.

Greed yellow—sand.
Greed purple.
Greed white. (Fire.)

There Is Only One Body

Two bodies of water
need the same thing for satisfaction—

you can be full yet empty:
when your constitution has clarity but contains no life,

and you can be both empty and full
only when you have room in all that self for other.

But how to be filled?

If someone gives you a fish, you can eat for a day;
if someone teaches you to fish, you can eat until

the stream's diverted or poisoned
or overfished or dried.

Two bodies of water, one human, one ocean:
one wholeness and the same way to it.

Until the stream's diverted or poisoned or overfished or dried.

Lessons from Mom for the Beach

The proper way to pee on yourself:
can you get to a secluded area?
If yes: go to the secluded area
and skip to stanza three.

If no: do you have a few friends that can stand
around you and hold towels? If yes: arrange
the friends and towels around you. (If no: lean
forward and drape a towel over your rear end.)

Now that you are in privacy,
is the area in need of neutralization
below the waist? If yes: skip a line.
If no: skip to the next "if no:".

Is the sting on the inside of the leg? If yes: fold
the affected leg under you and angle the leg
until the stream, when released, is positioned
over the affected area. If no: is there a cup or bucket

nearby? If yes: grab it and position it between
your legs. If it's not yours, deal with the
consequences later by informing the owner
that urine is sterile. You have a short window

of time before the pain reaches black-out
levels. If no bucket: cup your hands,
one at a time, to harvest as much of the stream
as possible to slather on the affected area.

When you are in position, release the
stream. Continue administration as long
as you can, even after the pain subsides.
Healing needs more time than relief.

The Secret Life of a Tween Scuba Diver

your limit: how much air you can carry on your back
every night dive I've done so far, my tank has come unstrapped.

The first time, my dive buddy—my dad—flailed his arms
until he got me standing on the bottom, breathing very lightly.

so I didn't start floating away until he could fix whatever
was wrong. That first time, when he had to stand on my shoulde

while he wrangled my tank back on, I was too freaked out to for
any hypotheses about what the heck was happening. Now,

my dad just flashes me a one-handed version of the internation
choking symbol and I know to start sinking.

your favorite: chasing after whatever flits into your flashlight bea
every kid who's scared of the dark is totally right: the world

is not the world at night. It so easily is whatever you think
it is. Like, this one dive, the second of that night, I was draggir

my light all over the place as soon as I found some coral and a roc
blinked at me. Rockfish, I thought. Naturally. I kick up close

so I can poke around, moving so, so slow and only from the kne
down not because I think I'm going to scare the fish—I'm the o

way, way out of my element here—but because every move
underwater at night ripples cold throughout the whole you.

your allergy: good to know; fancy places use it as food dye.
the blinking rock is not a rockfish. Rockfish do not have ink

they can squirt at you as they swim angrily away, leaving you
first just shaking from the adrenaline shot—
okay, I deserved that—

but then face-swelling hard against your mask
and a fire on your skin you've never felt on Earth.
Never been great at staying with my dive buddy,

who's used his entire tank in a single gulp
when I've disappeared before, I'm sure, and now,
no time to find him. No time for a safety stop, either.

The only diving rule I've never broken: never hold your breath.
I screamed the whole 60 feet to the surface
but not even I could hear it.

your secret: some octopuses look happy; most looked pissed off
I haven't taken Spanish yet—this is in Mexico, where the rules

are that you have to have a Mexican divemaster
and an American divemaster on every dive trip—
but even if I did, I don't know what happened.

The dive-boat captain has to cut my mask off my face
to get circulation back. My dad shoots out of the water
as soon as my cheeks swell enough to close my eyes

and throws off his vest as he runs to me. He almost steps on the
octopus that splats like a pile of jelly with legs to the deck. The
crewman shouts

what I now know to be "hold your breath" and dumps vinegar
over my head. My eyes are barely open before my dad hugs me
and
whispers *don't tell your mother.*

Shootings, Each A Mile Away

A gunshot is a word that needs no translation. Stop.
   Parents had to get us kids after seven hours of lockdown.
   The scariest thing about death
   is how far from home you seem to go

   and there are so many unknown things to be sad about.
On the drive home, the lion hide–colored leaves look like
hectically severed bird wings on the bushes.
The juniper orbs look like a candy trail for a trusting kid.

Showing a detour around the execution chamber at Columbine
High School, down the street from my middle school,
the traffic cones' orange is chemical,
rude against the green of what's been spared road paste.

   I see my first very white fire hydrant as we pass
   the police-clogged school, where a sheriff
   floods each car with his silver flashlight
   whose handle could double as a club.

   I bow my head and when I look up,
   I see more white hydrants—they are not white;
they are yellow encased in hard, white robes,
arms out in a T like the memorial crosses

we'll erect and two of which will be burned
every year now on the anniversary—
as we stop-and-go past the cautioned-off scene.
   When we heard the explosions,

a swooned sun was belly up in past-tense red
   is why the clearest indication of how

I'm doing is still to ask me how's the weather.
Is the sun we've not seen for days impotent behind the clouds?

Abusive? Or does it shine lucidly, like an officer's torch?
Questions are for when you're older.
I think aren't we listening—
I wanted a love, I think, I wanted a love that will

make me realize any hope I had before it
was incomplete. Love kills what it needs,
I know, like when you fight afraid
which is so far from fighting fear—

but how to tend to this empty barrel, this empty head?
    Those 15 empty desks in US History class up the road,
    these two empty chairs at youth group the very next evening?
    The news showing—over and over—the half limp boy falling

    from a shattered window into the arms of frazzled medics?
The referencing of it—over and over—after every subsequent
scourge; so often that when I saw the word uncapitalized for the first
time years later, I didn't know the word? (It is a thin-winged, blue

and white flower, the official one of my home state.)
I am older. I live in another state by another scene engulfed
in the same Do-Not-Enter tape and spinning lights and hammering
sounds that pound my head down, down,

stop. I don't think, I don't think aren't we listening anymore.
God. We are not. We are the tiniest blue hummingbird
in all that ever was—in a whittled cage with its Coliseum bars,
locked iridescent gate and missing recompense—golden as silence.

Headstone

We are asked to peel potatoes.
We are told to put the skins,
which my sister can produce in a single
spiral strip, into a dented metal bowl
between us.

We will save them for soup.
I think. I do not think the popular thing is true;
death is not "just a part of life."
My sister finishes flaying her spuds, bounds off
 into the unmowed yard.

It is harder than that;
It is not as if life and death amicably separated
like an out-of-love couple so that they may find
 more satisfying companions.

Dad reaches inside for breath enough to call his youngest back
but she's off into hay and tresses of what's left of daylight
blonde like Mom was even up to this day last year.
My sister will not remember. I will not outlive my grief.
When Mom laughed, she laughed from her soul, they said.

I remember it like that now, growing in a room
like the steam from her scrumptious kitchen magic.
I will not outlive my grief.
But maybe it is not impossible to live;
extremes can exist back to back.

I give you the zebra, sunset, a naked potato
clutched in accidentally sliced fingers. Dad is still looking
past where his girl disappeared to the yard of stones
displaying summaries of entire lives. Death is apart from life,
he whispers, grazing the pane with his fingertips.
It will always be as hard as that.

Healing Is So Small

The ocean is a seed
on a low, coughing land
and what does that mean
what does that mean
for us who are the salt
of the earth?

I know what it means
for those who are the light—
show the way, not yourself—
but do those
who are the salt
preserve or dissolve?

Young For Now

They, the girls, braid each other's hair, slide on sandals
and grab thin, purple jackets they won't need for the summer outside

Below a furious drum of sun in skinny clouds,
color-drained weeds faint like discarded bits of sewing thread.

The stream is still trying, drooling down the hills to the heat-packed
stables. The horses are having more difficult births.

All the adults comment on how hot everything is,
how everything is beaten with heat. How neglected they feel by rain

When Uncle Joe, heat-worn, comes looking for help
with the harvest, the girls take their books and run by the brook

and sit, feeding the mosquitos. The world is a sea of flesh.
They giggle and squirm, till the younger one jumps up, runs to the water

grabs the rope, swings across. The other eyes the current,
stays on shore, braces while her sister pendulums

over frigid brook and fills the moment with glee.
Who will be in trouble if the rope, the moment, breaks?

They forget about their books, though reading is a required
bodily function, run home at the first spot of dark.

They do not yet see the shortage of ponies.
They do not know they need to say goodbye.

So they don't. The world is open sea,
but not enough leagues will flush the need.

This Is What the Storm's All About

Children float in plastic tubs
by ruined keepsakes heaped high.

An Angry Cat meme goes viral.

Apocalypse means a stripping away.
New Orleans, Houston, Florida, The Eastern Seaboard,
Puerto Rico's full of grit now.

Take great pride in being ready to help.

Families, crouching, huddle on their roofs,
knowing why but not how to protect their young.

We will not leave our places of refuge the same.

Healthy babies, though, have long since
become a memory for some of our women.

Everything on the water bobbles over barriers without ID.

A sign, hard to say if damaged: *Spirit: Free*
with the $100 purchase of any brand-name shoe.

Love In The Injustice Age

is when you know someone so well
you could be her scream.

Tia and I, we have caught a glimpse
of our extinction; we are hunting it down.

We build peace with justice, Tia and I.
She cracks jokes like belts and I dig like an insult

and the scant trees seize in the wind.
We make this ditch with pickaxes

and fear and sick hope and just us.
We are trying to prevent wasteland—

place where no mystery can live—at least *somewhere*—
and so we have to dig. Past dirt, through

the fat bones of old trees, below
water tables, screaming with life.

Barrier. But we must find what everyone
will believe is worth saving.

Tia shares personal opinions about love
and cancer. I press her to keep digging with me.

We must find something gold for humanity
and we must find it here. We do stop—

for snacks, for sleep, to watch darkened light
plunder the growing thunderheads.

Birds fly in off the tsunamic sea that is hooked
like a rubber band around God's thumb.

'Do you hear that sound?' Tia asks, leaning
her shovel into juicy soil. Nothing from the birds

but the moon, small but good shepherd, yelps
against our never-dulled blades. Frogs, the ones

we haven't dissected in our hurry, waddlecrawl
across sticky leaves we've tossed aside.

Blades buzz in the sepia breeze. Tia gets to the ground,
wrists, elbows, triceps, ear. "Here." She handprints

the pulped dirt. "Here." I see the scream—
blue holes in my vision—before I feel it gash my throat.

Tia buries her face in the slit shoulder of earth.
It is painful to believe that every rock is sacred because

nothing survives love.

First 9a–5+!

Those were the days! Almost all of them wasted
with expectation of all the time in the world.
Nights skewered by buzzing suns on metal trees.
Waiting for the bus shrink-wrapped in directionless bliss.

Procrastination is the flowering of the belief in infinite lifespans.
I kept pushing off my Real Work, finding my Why,
certain as only the young can be that this shit employment
is just a starter job.

It's fine that it's meaningless. The world is my oyster!
I am a member of the Participation Trophy generation.
I buy my pistachios shelled.
I have no clue how to crack a clam.

Remember the sounds, look at the faces.
I coach myself to stay present as I multitask
commute as exercise, half listening to old-timey rock
my father strove to teach me to love,
shoulder sore under purseweight.

Looking back is a favorite pastime of the regretful—
no dancing partner keeps time better that what you never did,
like that two-steps-forward-one-step-back addiction
to the striving to spin something of emptiness

if only you weren't so tired already.

If I were time,

people would marvel
at how much of me had passed without their noticing,

how both long and scarce I am,
how only I have the balm for some wounds,

only I can change things likes minds or hearts
but I myself don't change.

Maybe this is why some seek ways to stop or even kill me.
You'd think I was the perfect lover, the way some talk about me—

they can never have enough.
But I'm searching for that one

who can enjoy me just as I am.
Empty, inert, needing help knowing what I'm made of.

Embrace the Homeless Woman Selling Papers

her gloveless hands presenting dusty news
her crisp brown eyes rising and quickly plummeting
to her graying sneakers with each squeaky swipe
of the automatic doors as shoppers exit,
heavy bags swinging from their elbows
this word in front of that word
that you hear yourself say to her

we suffer
when we believe in things
we do not understand

the outsideness of her world to you
that you can never know if you feel warmth
the way she does, too small for her thin,
dull-brown coat, and her body, especially her eyes
that it was you who needed the hug

and when we do not quite believe
in people, places or things,
it is not quite suffering

the creases clawing at the corners of her eyes
the smile she gives you as she tells you
about the slow death of her cat,
which was outside with her always,
and great on a leash without ever being trained
how you reach into and then out of yourself to get that hug

but if we are very certain
that a person, place or thing
is something else,

then we should use a metaphor—
like hugging that catless woman
is a very full grocery bag—then again,
what is a better metaphor for suffering
than itself standing on its own
two tired feet
holding you with its own two gloveless hands

First Love Never

When he said she said I should meet so and so,
I beat around many thorny bushes,

found and overturned many stones
but not much luck

let several cats out of their bags, though it depends,
I guess, on what you mean by bags

set more than two birds carefully back on their twisted bowls,
didn't touch their babies, anything at all, really,

besides the ruddy roses growing fiercely
from those barbed bushes

aching in the sun outcasting all shadow
before slumping on its wheel.

Dog Walking

To learn what new skin feels, walk
walk walk walk walk walk walk walk
in bad shoes lance a blister bad shoes
lance blister bad bad bad bad blister,
hold a sewing needle in a flame
hold hold hold hold hold hold me
though I am a flame and lance
the bad blister after you count count
count count count all the holds you seem
to have on your life love work friends
and holding all on hold hold hold count them
hold hold hold hold hold hold hold hold,
push out all the liquid it will hurt hurt hurt
hurt hurt but not as bad as having a soul
in a world that's losing losing losing losing
its, then clip clip clip with nail clippers
the bubble of old skin all away away away.
Expose to air until new layer of skin
plastic wraps wound. Wound will be shiny
as if wet well into next day.
Note: wound, unlike heart, will stop beating
and hurting after lanced, squeezed and exposed.

Morning Thrush

Can this be a good place to end: I found
the alarm clock to rouse the dead.
Not the writhing water
from our wedding-present kettle.
Not trying to carry it—all our mugs
are handleless—to the couch—
that's where the prettier table is.

Not noticing that our untidy
bathroom needs cleaned. Not the neck-jerking
look at the time. Not the unmade bed. Not
the unbrushed teeth. Not
my own howling alarm.

But I Am Still Connected To You

The water I walk over commuting
from my day job
cradles the moon, the face of a man whose aging
    will never stop.

Slender rain pinpricks his foamy cheeks and rounded jowls,
shatters as I walk through it into infinitesimal pools
on the shabby sidewalk all the way to home.
    It's swishing and tangling in branches

of the drama-queen weeping willow
    (I, too, want to cry and never stop)
I asked my dad to plant next to the greedy lilac
    I imported to my own garden from Pop's.

Is there a better way to honor passing eighty-three years
    on knees beside pews, among bees and peat and
painted petunias, all to lay fallow and eventually be remembered
    by no one in a listing world

that never stops? I could have paused in my white of orbit,
    tended the lilac with him while it was still his,
taken my here and there to his here and now.
I only have these holes, a waft of budding, a dent of rainfall.

Hiking Kendall Katwalk

We were out in 50 degrees for 11 miles
and we came back wearing all the rain.

I thought it even in the moment as a right-on
metaphor for our marriage, not least because

I had refused to hike long, I had refused to hike cold
and I had refused to hike wet. But maybe I can do this.

Things we realized out on the trail
that might be useful: a wide-brim hat,

a towel, gaiters that cinch as small as one's actual
calf muscle, discernment of poison in berries,

knowing who steps aside when people need to pass.
We left our books at home; we had assumed

the terse 'hi' accompanying
a glare from the one hiker we saw

on our way down meant, 'Actually,
you're supposed to step to the side

for me.' We didn't know. The people
(in shorts? thin jackets with thin hoods

knotted tight around their thin chins?)
we passed on our way up all moved

for us. I'm glad none of them had kids
with them; my sadness hollows me

whenever I see children. It's not quite this:
what will be left for them? It's not quite this:

I miss young me. I wish I could remember her.
I trust there is good reason I don't.

Light: frail among the boulders surrounding us,
surrounded by beings who have trees

for bodies. We were half a mile from
the main attraction before we, frozen numb,

turned back. We didn't know. We couldn't operate
our zippers, open our water bottles (which was just

as well: it was too cold to squat in the bushes).
If we needed a swig, we could open our mouths and look up.

Maybe I can do this. I did like this long, freezing, wet hike,
as my husband kept reminding me. "You like this. You like this."

It was aggressively uncomfortable.
I'd never felt so alive, as they say, and I guess I did like it.

Still, the part of the dream that is not so easily dodged
wants to pitch its tent in a field of daisies coated in sun,

usually nowhere to be found. But maybe I can do this.
And I do. Until the sun finally offers me its jacket.

Sabbath

All aircraft except military were grounded for three days after two planes knocked down two buildings in New York City on 9/11/01. I was a sophomore in high school locked down—in history class—for a few hours on the day of the attack because the Columbine shooters had written about hijacking planes after escaping the epic police battle they dreamed about surviving and flying them into NYC (Columbine was less than ten minutes from my house, my high school and the middle school where I was during the massacre) and the first time I stepped outside after that, the wind felt like surgical blades.

I remember hearing something about how the ozone started to heal even in those 72 hours of no commercial flying.

Stop air travel into and out of just one country for just three days and the holes in the planet's protection begin to close. You could conclude, "That must be a pretty important country." Or you could conclude, "That must be a pretty powerful planet." Or even "Rest must be a pretty powerful thing." Up to you. Two relevant facts as you consider the options: 1) Outer space smells like gunpowder and barbecue. 2) The variables in how physicists calculate work are force, displacement and the extent
to which the force causes or hinders the displacement.

A/B Testing

                                    A planet,
                                pushed into
                            the black blanket
                              like a button,

                              life roiling around
                            on its thinnest layer
                              amid smoke from
                        the nostrils of volcanoes

                            dense blasts of weather,
                              pressure to bloom
                          beyond simple survival,
"Push record."   now rolling full circle

                                back to questions
My assistant,

                                    of survival.
DataHead 12-06.1,

                                    Preservation:
complies

                          is it about more than data?

and the only camera

                                    The only ship
on the whole ship

                              in the known darkness
that wasn't rolling

                            to carry the bytes for life
begins gobbling

                                is...sinking is not

atmospheric pressure,

soil density,

population spreads

per country –

an endless list

of measures—

bit by planetary bit.

The pictures take

approximately 12.072

minutes to complete.

The moment it does,

we count to ten.

My turn to push a button.

Smoke curls around Africa,

the Atlantic splits in two,

then five, then ten,

continents go ash, millions

the word, for there truly

is no up or down.

No wonder the captains

do not know right or wrong.

An endless list

of things that could go wrong

absorb their time

like a hydrocarbon-flooded

atmosphere chugs sunlight.

It takes years,

but by the time

you notice,

you may not have time

to debate their origin.

Cape Town will be out

of water, Bangladesh

of miles of skin go liquid

at a rate DataHead 12.06-1's

glass better be capturing

through the expanding rings

of red and scream and energy

transfer and all we felt is a tiny,

brief recoil under our thumb?

and San Francisco

will be under it.

But big brothers beat

up the bullies; technology

saves

(the way a good guy

with a gun saves).

NICU: Room 226

Day one had been bloodless;
you, having come from so far (from all
the way inside), are already far away

by the transfusion of night. Do you fear
you are a member of the generation that will
have to see the end of the story?

I fumble affixing the Do Not Resuscitate
sign to your door. Tubeage ferrets good in/bad out
of your little liver, stomach, hard gem

of a heart. Broken beepery blares
oxygen levels, heartbeats per minute.

Precise young nurses poke in close
enough to stroke the skin of your new soul.
The incubator spills jaundice-yellow light.

The next morning, the sun shreds clouds
like they're tissues and the light coming
down is miracle-grade white.

It Takes Two

The EPA's headquarters flooded again last night.
It doesn't even take a hurricane anymore.
We have to meet in the windowless
room on the 8th floor with the fake Jade
the new girl keeps watering.
   "We've agreed on what to fill the space
on the website with now that we've taken down the
CC." Climate crisis?, climate change?, climate compatibility?,
—many options here...corruption, calamity, probably
not cooling,
   but that's not why we abbreviate. "Material from
the website: Guidelines for an agreement with Earth."
Apparently 'we' think she's not really been keeping
up her end of the bargain – the floods and fires, sometimes
at the same time in different parts of the same state;
and quakes where there are no plates and blizzards
in Tampa and whatnot.
   We apparently propose the following guidelines, in rough
order:
1) Give clearer warning signs about inclement weather.
(You did before). We can't read your mind, Mother.
Relatedly, 2) tell us what you need: use your words.
Tantrums are counterproductive.
3) Cease and desist on the spotty or decreased yields.
Water and soil should always equal food. Finally,
4) Take more responsibility. Who just lets themselves get
assaulted?

Birthday

These thirties shouldn't be mine yet.
I used to wait for them like I waited for
Christmas morning.

Then, a few years ago, I noticed Santa's skeins
of white hair, his rugose forehead,
that his reindeer would have to drop him

off right by the chimney so he didn't have
far to walk, just like we do with my fragile
grandmother.

Age suddenly seems impossible – to get
and to live with, even as Christmas started
to crawl up quicker every year.

This last one – I almost missed it.
I have been executing these extraordinary
disciplines of eating, bathing, breathing,

apparently at Godspeed – how else would I have
gotten here so fast, broken so soon
my pinky-promise to myself that,

as I impatiently grew up, I would never get old?
I would accomplish this by always crawling
in the car head first not sliding in sideways;

always cannonballing into the pool
not sliding in slowly like you see moms
doing at the edges; always chewing gum

and always trembling with bright eyes through each day
between December 1st and the morning where
all you've ever wanted was waiting for you

under a sagging fan of pine. The last year I tried
to keep this tinsel-tinged holiday spirit
until my birthday at the end of February was my 29th.

Thirties, from this close up, looks less
like a pile of gifts under a bright tree
and more like a jaw ache (no Wrigley's for me)

or a square of maybe gorgeous
but very cold water: I've missed
the chance to slide in inch by inch.

The Roman Name for Time

Climate shifting makes time molten
for a human. For a photon, time does not move.

Does 'to be in the light' mean
'to see everything at once'?

How much would we leave done,
how much would we refuse to undo?

Everything happens at once
because everything is in the same place.

And yet, you can either know where you are
or how fast you're moving. Not both:

you're a wave and particle.
All matter is.

Everything that matters is, is, is
in the same place.

We miss it. We glimpse it. We slip from it.
We do not decide everything that matters.

I have to laugh. I have to
laugh to protect the guilty.

If you are in the light, you are not the light.
And if you are the light, it is time that is still,

you are not. But, oh, is it yet dark.
Time is running.

Everything is not still here, but everything
that is still here still matters. Even if no one is looking.

Child Raising

We're on a walk in our neighborhood
past petunias and perfect
little lawn swatches, me and Bull—
and let me just say that dogs can talk
a mean, ammoniac slick around their subjects,
especially 'traitors' who withheld treats that morning—

and the small one, all fenugreek freckles
and a memory you only hear about on the news.
She repeats my explanation to Bull about his need
to lose weight verbatim down to the affect.
She sang a song I sang when I thought she was asleep.

She's naming the flowers all the same
primal sigh of awe. Bull barrel-chests down
the excursus of gravel lining our mottled-petal-free
sidewalk delineating (our) weeded, trimmed plot
from (not our) toy-strewn lawns with balding spots.

Bull pulls as I think: how to teach big one
to wait, small one to purge—not nourishment,
but its adversary: the beauty yardsticks, the ravages
of scholastic approval, ipecacic relationships.
She's not shown me she knows anything

about any of this yet. For now, it's all whole
smiles and stepping over cracks
and flower fawning while I strain hard against all this leash.

The Park with Kids

On the grass, face to the sky:
what if that cloud really is
a giant smile or a whale or a spaceship

wondering what we really are?
What if the magic is real?
What if the world they see

adrift above is just as they see it?
The horses and houses and hearts here with us
on the ground are like them: still growing, going shortly.

Glass Hour

Kids eat dirt. They don't know
that they have a limited time
to be infinite. This is okay:
tomorrow will take most of forever

to claw its way to us and start over again.
Mountains pile up on young tongues,
then worlds on older shoulders
as they arc back into earth with us.

Children fill their mouths with dust.
It is beautiful:
they don't know it's what they are.
Nothing but a minute,

sticky with what-is-all-this
reverence for no more
than a minute,
forever if you're chewing mud.

Stamp

If you stop
your step
on a smoothed walk

for only a breath
and drop
your eyes,

you might
not notice
small rises

or pokes of pink
furry stitches
of green

in the separations:
slight signs

that we do not own
cannot leash
this place we've paved.

Physics

Was Jesus materializing inside a locked room
a 'miracle' of probability?

Every single thing is almost really nothing
and yet there are collisions.

So the roiling emptiness I contain
corresponds to something real!

Affirming. But what I cannot bear, then,
is that all this stuff we call beauty is mask.

We may see splendor atop all bare space,
but impact is no intimacy.

When Do Death and Destruction Break?

Sacred:
every eddy, home run, cat,
all flooring, seeds

rough air, boulders, ponytails,
sinkholes. It is hard to believe that every rock
is holy. It's pouring wind and flood.

I long for an earlier date of birth.
Old people, who in ancient times
did not walk fast, scuttle toward overhangs.

Sustaining:
crumpled dirt clapping as it hits wood
you spent weeks selecting

and then lacquering yourself
wearing a gas mask you stopped bothering
to take off each time you went outside.

Can you believe it? People
sit in boxes under false light all day
and we are working hard to live forever.

Grief:
lying in a growing pool of your own blood
after a vehicle crash

unable to decide whether to hope
to be close enough to the road so that headlights reveal you
or tires finish you off.

Resist this. Hurt, yes, as much as you can.
But wanting to die gives the thieves
permission to want you dead.

No One In My Culture Has My Disease

(This is how I express it to my husband.)
But he doesn't see, yet, the trouble
with remaking the world out of technology.
"Just think about the kinds of people

who would look good in binary," I strain.
Dictators, henchmen, murderers, industry captains.
(The skin of the earth is worth trillions.)
What will it take for us to think safely? is what I'm going for.

(Or: think about those who would disappear in duality).

Example: Gramma was a carpenter;
she built all the banks in town.
She taught me: look up through our Aspen
at the rind of winter sun and it will look

like the sky has freckles.
I saw the sky as a face and it changed me.
But I am the same person as the one who listened
to my grandmother tell her memories as stories.

Where we buried her, a bench with a plaque:
a respite for those who see beauty in all things.
I kick a rock, break the lake's picture of the pines
who go on standing together, keeping out a wind.

"The Hockey Stick is Broken,"

my spouse tells our kid, who's tracing a carbon graph
with her perfect little finger. "Your mom's got it deep
in her head that this spike at the end means trouble.
It's all I can do to redirect her to reality: God.

Finally, she wants to pray
the President won't take my job away
and I fold my hands arounds hers—
the blackness of my palms is just soot stains.

The president won't take my job away
because the President looks out for me—
the blackness of my palms is just soot stains.
You have heat in your homes because of me and

because the President looks out for me
without anything more intrusive than pride and duty.
You all have heat in your homes because of me and
the loyal men of this country who keep its shape

without anything more intrusive than pride and duty."
Finally, my kid wanted to pray for
the loyal men of this country who keep its shape
and I folded my hands around hers.

Items May Have Shifted During the Fight

If you're not from the East Coast of the US
(I'm not), it will feel like you're in a dish-
washer if you go there. If you're not from
Colorado (I am), your nose will crack, may-

be bleed, if you go there. The boundary bet-
ween the two climates – you know by feel if
not by name or by sight that there is one – has
shifted 140 miles in 100 years, from 100th

meridian to almost 98th meridian.[1] This means
Colorado's desert-esque heat and dryness, both of
which I have missed my decade-plus stay in the Pacific
Northwest will reach the Mississippi. This means the air

will be lighter in more and more parts of the
country. This means that things like clothes and stuffed
animals will dry—rather than mold—if you set them out over-
night. This means humans won't have to shovel snow as often to get

to work. Really, what this means is this: people and infra-
structure exist to the east; in the west, population is sparse;
crops need to be arid-resistant. I used to joke that we don't
have water where I'm from, that what does grow there fries and dies

by August and has to start all over again every year. Farms
will need to become bigger to survive, and have to grow more
wheat and large stretches of cropland may fail altogether. Water
supplies could become a problem for more urban areas like my sweet
Denver: the line will not stop moving, like a squeegee across my whol-

---

[1] https://www.usatoday.com/story/news/nation/2018/04/13/climate-boundary-
shifts-140-miles- global-warming/514911002/

America, This Is Your Nobody

My home is made of planks
covered by a monsoon-blue tarp
and the world is so big and is over so soon.

My school is a needy forest
under a duck-footed bridge and the seasons
fall off it to their deaths too soon.

My job is practicing holding my breath
while pointing at penitent birds
and I always let a few slip by uncounted.

My heart is made up of thunderstorms
and holes bigger than fists. I don't have shoes;
I have strong feet and straight toes.

Self Care

In the next session with our therapist,
I report that he steps on my feet
all the time.

"So the best thing to do would be
to keep your feet out of the way."
We spend

the rest of the session talking about
how to support him in feeling safe
to be honest.

She asks how my feet feel a week later.
"Fine, but my neck hurts from staring
at the ground,"

the kicked-shitless earth, "all the time."
"It might help to alternate looking up and down."
It might.

Like how it might help the earth not to freely
bleed when punctured or to release her chokehold
on carbon

instead of hoarding it the way the wounded
hoard fear: unconsciously and as part of a lethal
cycle.

Nothing Is the Convenient Interpretation

(And a by-product of convenience,
it turns out, is mass death.)

How it feels to be on the earth
is asleep.

The earth, I mean.
Pins and needles.
The earth is full.

Clapback. Mic drop. Amen.
Amen?

The earth does not say amen.
Drill here. Pave here. Here. Here. Here here.

The body of the earth was a sink,
now a hole. Unending

but not unendable.

It is clearcut. Which is pain.
What does the earth say?

When Discussing the Weather Is Still Considered Small Talk

So you know how we bury people
after they die, my daughter asks me.

It's cold for summer. We forgo the lemonade.
I've climbed mountains alone. I don't know

the way to descend the despair one in time
always. Yeah, I tell my daughter. I know. Sun falls

like rain. The air is burning. Or maybe it's
my lungs. *Do you really know?* my daughter

says. I have stood at the base of mountains
at the feet of the sky and it was like they'd

never not known glory. But they are crumbling
before your eyes. Yes, baby, I tell my kid. Really.

I don't. Who is going to bury the earth? The least
we could do as we steal the world dry is be *satisfied*.

Guilt

Even if life is a hasty biochemical
agreement, it is a well-negotiated one.

I do not want to be alive
for the collapse of the world.

But goodness needs a hearing.
Dissolution deserves a vigil.

Light for the Blind
attending an open-casket service

Grief, you are like God: quite the giver.
I want to beg your day breaks its tarry.
So many, so much, is being lost.
Did you consider I am still a child?

But more might collapse
if you grant my plea.
so in this slow time, I ask for my trust
to receive its sight.

My childhood friend's stand-in vessel,
now this imposition of ashes,
means we can now only speak
what we do not know.

People who love acutely
have this habit of dying violently;
does everyone else simply shoulder
on their fill of emptiness?

Stiff suits, standing-room only
at the service. The light fresh-laundry
soft, buzzing like flies. Spears of too-soon
winter pierce the hot blanket of summer sky.

Emptiness so barren not even
an echo can survive.
I prayed the way my friend's
foolhardy hope taught me to pray:

Dear outside world, from the pending one:
the body is like the soul,
and the body, like God, likes the soul.

Some come by church; others come through the bars.
Whatever way, no avoiding the storm
with a mouth full of hate and rain.

No answer is the full light,
not even when God speaks artillery shells
and the grace smells like sweat.

Trees poured from sky that day;
everything was sound.
Everything is held back

as long as it can be and then is nowhere.
The headstone is chiseled,
my friend is now earth,

a bright disappearance.
Her museum is full of visits
and I pay homage to *stones*?

Negative Space

A world: a drop, a single serving,
rests in the multi-pierced blanket of the cosmos
and you did not grasp it.

A baby: a fullness, a future,
sticks to the wall of its curved world
and you did not find it.

You: not a rescuer but a created thing,
dared to take the world down to its studs
in the name of understanding it?

You: a vulnerability, a passing presence,
carved bones and fire and strange blood
from the belly of home and laid it over everything

everywhere: a territory, a conquered puddle,
spread so over with what you thought you made
that you could not discover it.

You Are the World of the Light

I am in a little shattered forest
that has a balding crown.
The sun is diving into my skin

and tumbling around, bumping its shins
on mini mitochondrial furniture,
flooding nervous canals.

Things you think will always be there,
will always be you. Faster than
the housekeepers and general contractors

can do their work, the rays trash the interior.
They don't leave a scratch on the surface, though.
Not even a blush. What you can see is perfect.

Everything is still smooth, and a white
that's shrill against the ribbed plate
of green that is this sprig in my hand.

The light in this leaf is the general contractor,
slowly building itself into these verdant corridors
these cords of wood, these brave congregations

that unknowingly know everything.
We don't ask the trees, though, how to change gleam
to height. We just wring them all the way out

and live empty in the empty hovels
we make with their bodies, pining, if not for more
light, then at least for our walls to talk.

We Are Not World Enders

Today I was accused of stealing my own identity.
I was the accuser.

Grief saw itself in my mirror,
I was riven silent.

Child, you are not the machine of yourself,
you are the ghost in you.

How do we learn humility?
That you are nothing special in the way you learn

you are nothing special?

I learned: the doors into the world—
work, relationships, love, meaning—

they are all on fire. The world itself.

Dear graduation speakers:
I wish I had not believed you.

"The world is your oyster"?

The world is fire. Or else dank quiet.
Undecodable celebration in the dark.

If you were a star

and you had strong vision during the COVID-19
spread, you would see the veins of the earth rock
fill with bright
and magnetize
the white and beige and gray and
blue specks that belong to them.[2]

You would see this rock's geologically recent blanket
of brown develop holes, dissipate completely in parts[3]
so you'd be able to see
all the way through
to a calm stretch of soil beginning
to natively stir as if jubilated by respite.

You would not know why, so you would
join the specks and the sea and the soil
in unfurled
revelry.

Of course, being a human
is being a star,
the vision

a blessed
gift

to open.

---

[2] https://www.cnbc.com/2020/03/18/photos-water-in-venice-italys-canals-clear-amid-covid-19-lockdown.html

[3] https://www.cnn.com/2020/03/17/health/china-air-pollution-coronavirus-deaths-intl/index.html

Ton As In Eschaton

The world cares for us but, because of us,
she drinks. She is beauty already,
before we clad her in stone.

The inhabit matters, how.
We make revolution like the sun
to embark – Mars! Does Saturn's moon have water?

We argue like the sea with shore,
but her prayers are planned for gardens,
for birds (not tweets).

"Let them not settle elsewhere
until they learn to need
a mother."

She undergoes so much under us,
but it is we who cannot cope
with everything that is here.

Crisis Projects

We are ExxonMobil, the largest publicly
traded energy company on Earth and the premier
petroleum and petrochemical team.

              Here at Crisis Diversion, we take referrals
              from hospitals, jails and the police.
         We can only welcome two new clients a shift

We are committed to superior performance,
impeccable operation outcomes
and perpetual returns for our stakeholders.

                 as we serve the most vulnerable,
           not necessarily the most well-behaved.
         We meet clients wherever they are

At Exxon, we affirm diversity: we conduct business
in almost every corner of the globe, which necessitates
continually updating our knowledge of culture.

          and believe in the capacity of everyone to heal.
       Our goal is to help clients identify their own strengths
          not necessarily what looks good to the outside

Our workforce is well-versed in servant leadership
and is constantly encouraged to contribute as fully and
productively as possible to their company's success goals.

              or what is the most efficient or productive.
       We keep the threshold for admission as low as possible:
             only those with rape convictions,

We weave personal metrics together with cultural competencies
for uninterruptible, worldwide service at every level.
No matter where you are. No matter what you need.

those not in behavioral control, and, most commonly, those
who are withdrawing from substances (we are just not medi-
cally equipped for this situation) are

As the biggest independent energy producer in the world,
we expect you to expect nothing less from us.
We are Exxon. You are Exxon. No one on the planet is

ineligible for services. This, substance use,
and the potential for withdrawal, is what disqualifies
Earth from services at Crisis Diversion.

Eclipse: August 21, 2017

We will be transcontinentally brought together,
for the first time in almost a century,
by being separated from the sun.

We will envy those of us
in darkness—they will get
to see Mars in the morning!

We will trust scientific predictions
enough to book hotels years in advance
so that we, too, can be in the dark

when it is supposed to be light.
We will stop our work and mill about
our offices above our cities,

count the rooftop parties and gatherings
on the top floors of parking garages,
the gathering of gatherings constellating

even just for 85% blockage. Streets clog.
The temperature falls. Goosebumps. Tears.
Totality.

"The greatest moment of my life next to having kids,"
a woman says on the news later. The kids:
"It was really cool." One boy, not aware of the camera:

"Isn't living on earth totality?"

R(evolution)

You are Brothers now,
Can you dig(itize) it?

Al(gorithm),
Ana(lytics), Ava(tar).

From sea(rch) to
shining sea(rch),

every person(a) has
a mic(rosoft),

each con(tent)
the cur(ation).

We are believers;
We are Br(other)s.

Partners in cri(me),
real time, zoom, zoom

to save the world
from the world.

I wish human destruction was like

the exuberantly rotting nurse logs
all along the trail of the last hike
I took my antsy rescue dogs
on before the season closed.

I left my little girls with their fevers
at their father's. I packed for what I knew.
I skirt a face-down river, flail as the marionettist
of my pack, dread that I wasn't born

a hundred years ago, farther from
the end of the world. I listen for the names
of things. The cold sizzles. Branches, bowed
as if laden with snow, weaken with their own

growing weight. How do I teach my girls about snow,
which dark isn't scary, what to do with wishes and love,
that the real fairy tale is when no one needs saving.
I excel at walks on the beach. We are in a woods.

We are in a woods because humans
aren't working. Human relationships aren't working.
I needed to be loved by someone who has failed;
that's not (yet) birds, gales, soil.

I hit dirt with my knees; my dogs look
crazy at me. Cups of earth in my hands,
dirt on my dogs' tongues. I hold their faces,
kiss them sorry, sorry. I'm so sorry.

This Is My Body, Broken for Who?

"What do we think? God left the oven on
and hasn't come back from work yet?"
I heard my own voice shout, startling me
awake. I'm in bed and my big toe,

the one I destroyed right before my first
trip to Europe as a teenager, is pulsing
pain with every heartbeat. I start brain-
storming ways to stop my heart, which

freaks it out and makes it pound faster.
Can they do toe replacements yet?
My mom had her hip done fairly easily years ago
but that was for a genetically malformed socket.

This toe problem is just how I discovered
self-harm. I'd clipped it too short, trapped
the edge of the skin attaching the nail
to the nail bed between the blades

of the clippers and yanked until I got it all,
even though it bled instantly and for two days.
I didn't know what I was doing.
But it felt a distraction I mistook for relief;

the best part was, I could hide it.
I filed my pinky toenails until they bled and
then kept going until I saw the lightning
I felt at the end of my body.

The sheet grazes my toe and I see
that same lightning from years ago.
It's been a while since this happened.
It's like phantom pain, only the thing

that's gone isn't made of flesh. It's made
of peace. So I resist the push for doing away
with the bone-and-blood substrates in favor
of human-created ones because human beings,

human bodies, have a rightful place here, though
we insist on bringing chaos out of order
And because the materials that will help
us leave our bodies and still live feel nothing.

British Columbia Burns, Summer 2017

Damn, this smoke is weird.
—Facebook post
Yes, it is weird. Like, not normal.
As in, don't wait for things to just go back to "normal."
—Reply

Downtown Seattle looks groggy,
like it's still waking up from a hard night's rest.
I thought the chalky haze that stung
my eyes—smoke can burn like fire—

somehow related to the record-setting heat
predicted for the first week of August in the
Pacific Northwest, currently panting from weeks
of drought—*less*, not *no*, rain;

in some parts, over 105 degrees.

But it's *harder* to sleep when it's hot.
And then the increase in pulmonary events,
advisories to avoid strenuous exercise outside,
all we are coming to just accept from the ghost

of a vaporized forest. Almost 7,000 people in Canada

have been evacuated so far; if you are vulnerable
in Oregon, you may be asked to leave as well:
small children, those aged over 65,
heart patients, the pregnant.

It's actually because of rain that fires
can get so bad: overly wet winters led to
an abundance of vegetation—friable fruit
in the burning eyes of fire. For days and days,

I have to close mine to the world.

The 8th Plague

The Book of Exodus (in the Old Testament)
has it this way: God inflicted ten calamities
on the nation of Egypt to persuade Pharaoh

to release God's people from slavery
even though God was preventing Pharaoh
from freeing God's people.

This sounds like human logic. And the plagues
aren't in any sort of discernable order, either.
They don't strike alphabetically or by subject

matter or by height or in order of least bad
to worst. Death of the firstborn does seem
like the worst to me – I'd have been a goner –

but boils, the 6th plague, seems worse than
turning water into blood, which "God" "does"
first. That's just creepy.

And the one with the locusts. Did God send a billion
bugs from heaven or is swarming the kind of thing
locusts do? Locusts are usually solitary

unless there's a drought followed by rapid vegetation
growth. The serotonin release this triggers
causes these introverts to get gregarious, breed

like mad and horde. Sure, this can instigate economic
and agriculture damage, but it's been happening
for thousands of years wherever locusts live.

I sympathize with Scripture writers, though.
When I'm facing powers far beyond my puny
control that are making me miserable,

the first thing I do, usually, is hurl a plague
of screams at every place I think God is
and especially in every place I think God is not.

Pile Up

Have you ever hit an animal with your car?
You know the sound of flesh and fear
against dumb, dead metal.

And you can't just leave the thing—
in our case a vixen—if it's alive.
You have to show her mercy if she won't live

and kill her. That's a hard call to make,
even if you've made it a thousand times.
Most lore about foxes is false—

they can't breed with dogs (different
chromosome numbers), they don't kill
for fun, they don't kill on accident.

They don't have superpowers, at least
our vixen didn't. She was DOA, or DOOA:
dead on *our* arrival. Sometimes it's not hard

to tell, but it's still hard. Sometimes,
it is hard to tell if they'll make it or not.
In our case: no question not.

You are supposed to learn to stop asking why.
You have to. Why this fox and not another?
You'll go mad. But I ask now as a small eulogy,

its size proportional to my knowledge
of this particular vixen. I ask why
the way owls ask who as I pinch

the tail fur of the vixen and drag it
to the side of the road. A couple of teens
out for a joy ride laugh at the sad mom

wasting her time with a dead fox, driving
her kids in the car crazy and twitching
as mange-bearing tics boing up her arm.

People don't like that there is dying.
I wonder if our collision with mortality
will leave us smeared on our roads

or bounced off in ditches dug, most likely,
by prisoners on work-crew duty.
Will we even feel it? Will we be the dumb, dead metal?

And who will drag us out of the way
of the parliament of fleshless operations
bringing up the beginning and the ending?

Alligator Proof

alligators are intelligent;
for one, they show great restraint

their primary prey is the wood duck;
they might float steadily just below the surface near one for an hour

alligators transport their babies in their U-shaped mouths;
when things get scary, they snap them safe

wood ducks have squat beaks that cannot snap;
orange and brown tipped or dull, depending on sex

male wood ducks have painted jowls and green iridescent mullets;
they always look surprised or tired

females can hide on brown water by sitting very still;
slender blue striping their wings' ends

alligators can rise without a ripple; only their eyes
break the surface—a human can scare an alligator off

if a wood duck lives through its first attack
it is alligator-proof from then on

this is what researchers observe over and over
still without a theory of how fragility defeats monsters

γλυπτός ὀδούς

—roughly: grooved tooth sculpture—
the Glyptodon was, some evidence suggests,
driven to extinction by humans thousands of years
before the invention of the English language,

which is impressive because picture
a more heavily-armored armadillo
the size of a Volkswagen and you've got
a Glyptodon. Also, as the climate deniers

like to say, this has been going on for
centuries, by which they mean climate change,
human-driven or otherwise, but by which
I mean human-driven extinction.

But back to the less controversial,
theoretical stuff. Seven-pound femurs
and tail parts were found in the 1820s
but it wasn't until his 1837 memoir

on Brazilian fauna when one Dr. Lund
identified the remains as part of a new genus.
Humans fought about what to name
the creature. Glyptodons fought each other

with their tails, humans think, rather than
other creatures, because of its flexible sections.
Physics and math tells zoologists that Glyptodon
tails could break Glyptodon carapaces,

which look up close like mosaics of tiny, white, flattened
barnacles arranged like tiles on a bathroom floor.
Artists' renderings of them are much cuter than
you'd expect after looking at the skeleton, which is

one of those things humans have to keep learning,
I guess: we hold hands and sing that, underneath,
we're all the same, or chant that it's what inside that counts.
True enough, but most underlying structures look haunted bare.

End After End

Time is not like a book
but more like grief
because it can go backwards
and it
grief
is the language there aren't words in
because it
grief
turns the tongue into an eraser

I read for the relief of chronology
watch the sea unfold its scrolls
on sharp rocks young and old
on recessing coastlines
on surfers
who have to be in the middle of everything
and it
the sea
gets close in on their shoulders

the close that is more than curiosity
is consumption, actually
and really
like time like grief
not like Ping-Pong
not like pinball
because you are alone
without an oar in it
grief maybe time
they both close in on your shoulders

the close that is more
always wants more
and it
the more

finds a way to surf on top of all
your desires
your white-knuckle strength
your sins your books the oceans
who shrug their shoulders
unless you can break their spines
with your tiny paddle hands

The Great Glass Party

We all want to be surrounded by ravishing.

But we are alive in the magic of *this* world,
which is whenever the castle,
however the hill.

It is time to celebrate that everything is connected.

Everything that is still here, everything that is not,
whatever the marring, whichever the color,
matter matters matter.

Life used to be the kind of uncertain that made the alive curious.

Paint is real, trees are real, lies are real, singing is real,
assault is real, love is real, cats are real, the truth is real,
rain is real, bombs are real, hope is, too.

Everything was always glass.

A Divorce Decree

My marriage was a mirage
the way wood chips mirage a forest:

you think there's something real there.
You think, *wood is softer than concrete*

so if I fall, ah, what the hell? You keep
playing even though you are alone

and every other relationship you see
is between adults who catch each other.

Actually, that's exactly right:
wood chips are dead forest

that are soft (as in, not strong)
and smell living. But they are dead.

Okay, so it's not actually exact.
My marriage was never living.

Only dead. Only dead.

The day the final orders were filed
and put on public record

for all to see my failure—I didn't
even get the dignity of real dead-tree

paper because even the law has caught up
and is virtual now—

I did a happy dance while sobbing.
First time in my life I've done *that*.

I cried like I had just been born.
And that is exactly right: I had.

To Be Tacked on Corporate Doors

A bird stands in heaven.
Spring. Cold, still.

Taking the day one sky at a time.

Oh, how can I tell you?
The poets' birds are in the spotted light.

How deep the beats of wings,
how smooth the gusts that raise them.

Beauty. How can I tell you?
Spring cold.

The sky one day at a time.

Beauty still.
We humans belong here.

People of the Origin Need Apply

Before they all died, my forbearers—
as in, bearers (humans)—

hanged everything they loved
on a mercilessly connected network

of lines, binary (black-or-white) then
 supra-binary (black-and-white) information.

Spiderwebs were stronger than the wires
that powered everything about their life,

then everything about them, before harvesting
then coffining all that was glory and free and love

about what had flowered the globe as life
(and maybe—but maybe not—the hope for a later redo).

To The Invisible

I am in a bar, explaining myself to Death,
who sips a Dark and Stormy.

She is painted up—turquoise eye shadow, rose cheekbones,
lustrous lavender lips—like she will never break apart.

Clutching a back-of-the-envelope set of notes,
a real mongrel of a to-do list, she affirms she has come

quickly, but at least she will be staying forever.
For a while, this is the only thing she says.

She does not mourn those I am reminding her
she clobbered long ago, too soon. She does not

answer my questions. She sips her drink,
neither smiling nor not and then checks her list.

She sees my ex-husband at the top—sighs—"an accountant for
every mystic"—then my best friend, who crossed himself off.

She catches my hand—I'm in the middle of a sentence
about a baby girl whom she permitted only one

great and fragile breath. She does not offer to pay
for the drinks. We stand. She starts to lead and I follow

until we're out under an expensive-looking black
cloth of sky, which shows white

in expertly positioned punctures. When I step ahead,
she catches my other hand, which I try to tug back only once.

Her gold-lined eyes dart from side to side and widen,
recently-plucked brows furrowing. I pity her. Even as she never

leaves, she will keep coming back, looking for a mirror,
the only way to tell if her mascara is running.

How to Talk About the Weather

child::adult as work::mature
ongoing::creation as loved::literature

fear::love as hate::hope
doubt::faith as rescue::rope?

soul::body as body::water
shadow::light as planet::fodder

love::fear as money::worth
Earth::multitude as living::birth

planet::fodder as other::rival
crisis::climate as _____::Survival

Acknowledgments

My sincere thanks goes to Cornerstone Press for giving this collection a beautiful home: Dr. Ross Tangedal, Director and Publisher, for accepting and publishing this work; Brett Hill, editorial director, and Maria Scherer, managing editor, for getting these poems ready to be published, and Julia Kaufman, production editor, for going several rounds with me on the cover design to get it just right.

Speaking of design, Katherine DiZio is the only creative director and designer who has been able to capture who I am in visual form. She has become a fast friend and has taught me so much about ethical, respectful design as well as how to powerfully and visually connect with your readers (not to mention given me permission to be my quirky self).

As have my longtime friends Keith and Ari. You have been active and steadfast champions of my writing, God bless you. Brittney, Brooke, and Kenny, you have also supported me all the way; my deepest gratitude to you. Thank you to Rebekah, the first to take me seriously as a writer all those years ago.

Thank you to NanaPop, who won't get to see this work but whose consistent presence in my life growing up has blessed me with so much material and love that will last the rest of my lifetime.

Thank you to my parents who did so well with me that my childhood dream of being an author stayed intact long enough to start coming true (and who had to wait three-plus decades to hear these words).

Thank you to my writers' group, who saw drafts of all of these poems and without whom they would not be fit to offer readers. Thank you for showing me what it looks like to care for other's words as much as my own.

Gratefully acknowledged are the following publications and contests, where earlier versions of particular poems were published or cited:

"Clay" was a top-ten finalist in *Blue Bonnet Review*'s annual poetry contest (January 22, 2016)

"Birthday" was the April Contest winner for CreativeInk's monthly writing contest (May 25, 2016)

"Glass Hour" appeared on *Algebra of Owls* (December 13, 2016)

"Embrace the Homeless Woman Selling Papers" was published as "Embracing the Homeless Woman Selling Papers" in *America Magazine* (March 21, 2017)

"Light for the Blind" appeared on *Bottlecap* (May 21, 2017)

"Shootings, Each a Mile Away" and "Headstone" (published as "Placing the Headstone"), published as "After Mom's Grave", appeared on *Sheila-Na-Gig* (July 16, 2017)

"Cementation" and "Young for Now" appear in *Long Division* (Finishing Line Press, September 2017).

"Young for Now" appeared on *The Same* (October 23, 2017)

"To The Invisible" appeared on *The Fenland Reed* (November 2, 2017)

"If I Were Time", published as "Time", appeared in *Spanida Literary Review* (January 26, 2018)

"Both Sides" appeared on *Blanket Sea* (April 16, 2018)

"How to Talk About the Weather" appeared in *Ibis Head Review* (June 2018)

"But I Am Still Connected To You" was published as "Perforation" in *Pangolin Review* (July 2018)

"Love in the Injustice Age" appeared in *Shantih Journal* (October 6, 2018)

"Negative Space" appeared in *borrowed solace* (Fall 2018)

"I wish human destruction was like" appeared in *Thimble Magazine* (March 22, 2019)

"Lessons from Mom" appeared in *8 Poems* (June 2019)

"Guilt" appeared in *Glintmoon* (September 25, 2019)

"A/B Testing" appeared in *Kissing Dynamite* (September 30, 2019)

"When Do Death and Destruction Break?" appeared in *Pedestal Magazine* (December 19, 2019)

"The 8th Plague" appeared in *8 Poems* (December 26, 2019)

"Dog Walking" appeared in *Comstock Review*'s (Fall/Winter 2019)

"I wish human destruction was like..." appeared in *Cordite Review* (February 2020)

"Green Room" appeared on *Lucky Jefferson* (May 1, 2020)

"Headstone" and "Remainder" appeared in *Gyroscope* (April 2021)

"Pile Up" appeared in *Channel* (April 2021)

"Physics" on *Plume Poetry* (May 1, 2021)

"(R)evolution" appeared in *Masque & Spectacle* (September 1, 2021)

"This is My Body, Broken For Who?" appeared in *Poetic Sun* (September 2021)

"Timber" appeared in *Cacti Fur* (October 2021)

MEGAN WILDHOOD is a neurodiverse writer from Colorado who strives to help readers who have a sense of invisibility finally feel seen. She is the author of the chapbook *Long Division* (2017), and her work has been published in *The Atlantic, Yes! Magazine, Mad in America, The Sun,* and elsewhere. Readers can learn more and get in touch at meganwildhood.com.

CPSIA information can be obtained
at www.ICGtesting.com
Printed in the USA
BVHW031114280423
663228BV00006B/209